# CONTENTS

Tough Task Rap 4

Brave Boy Rap 35

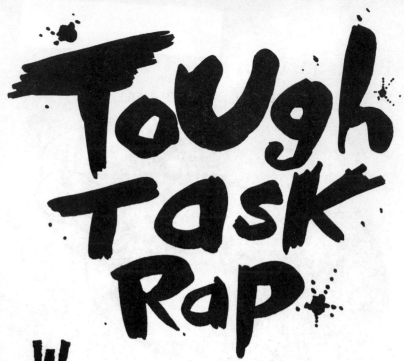

# Tough Task Rap

**W**elcome, folks,
to sunny Greece,
where holidays
are had in peace,
and dudes like you
can take it easy
on beaches (hot)
or mountains (breezy).

# Tony Mitton

# GROOVY GREEK HERO RAPS

## Illustrated by Martin Chatterton

ORCHARD BOOKS

*For Tim, Lewis, Auden and Isherwood*
*from all the Mitton-McKellars*

ORCHARD BOOKS
96 Leonard Street, London, EC2A 4XD
*Orchard Books Australia*
Unit 31/56 O'Riordan Street, Alexandria, NSW 2015
First published in Great Britain in 2000
First paperback edition 2001
Text © Tony Mitton 2000
Illustrations © Martin Chatterton 2000
The rights of Tony Mitton to be identified as the author
and Martin Chatterton as the illustrator of this work
have been asserted by them in accordance with the
Copyright, Designs and Patents Act, 1988.
A CIP catalogue record for this book is available
from the British Library.
ISBN 1 84121 797 2 (hardback)
ISBN 1 84121 799 9 (paperback)
1 3 5 7 9 10 8 6 4 2 (hardback)
1 3 5 7 9 10 8 6 4 2 (paperback)
Printed in Great Britain

But though this place
seems bound to charm you,
it once held creatures
who could harm you.
Heroes had to
chase them away,
so you could come
on holiday.

A very early
one of these
was hunky hero,
Heracles.

When Heracles
was just new-born,
he'd hardly had
the time to yawn,
when some mean goddess
in the sky
decided that
he'd have to die.

She sent two serpents
to his cot
to strangulate
the little tot.

Our hero held them
in his hands
and stretched them like
elastic bands.
He pulled them back,
then let them go
and flicked them out
the window - yo!

And from that day
he showed his skill
at finding things
to fight and kill.
(There was no shortage
in that age,
for horrid things
were all the rage.)

Now Heracles had
a cunning king
who got him doing
everything.
The king thought,
"While I have this man,
I'll use his muscle
all I can.

I'll tell him that
he'll get no rest
until he's passed
my little test,
then send him out
to fix or fight
the things round here
that just aren't right."

The king then made
a lengthy list
of bad things that
would not be missed!
Then meanly added
a thing or two
that really would
prove hard to do.

So now I'll tell them
one by one.
Yo! Are you hip?
The list's begun.

Task number one
took place near here.
A giant lion
was spreading fear.
But Heracles,
so bold and brave,
went striding straight
into its cave.

He grabbed its neck
and took a breath,
then squeezed the wretched
beast to death.

And when the fierce
lion was dead,
he wore its mane
upon his head.
The skin hung down
just like a cloak.
That *did* impress
the local folk!

Not far away
there lay a marsh.
It housed a serpent,
huge and harsh.

The Hydra was
this serpent's name.
Being horrid
was its game.
For if you went
too near that swamp,
its tail went *slash!*
Its jaws went *chomp!*

13

So here we are,
task number two.
The king said,

Just the job for you.
This Serpent's bound
to keep you busy.

(And true, it drove him
pretty dizzy.)
He tried to hack
the serpent dead.
But every time
he lopped a head
another two
grew in its place.
It really seemed
a hopeless case.

14

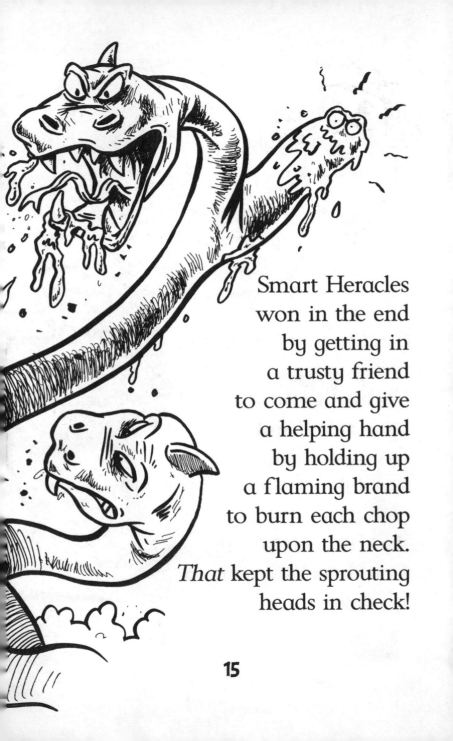

Smart Heracles
won in the end
by getting in
a trusty friend
to come and give
a helping hand
by holding up
a flaming brand
to burn each chop
upon the neck.
*That* kept the sprouting
heads in check!

And soon the serpent
lay there dead
without a single
hissing head.

This brings us to
tasks three and four,
to catch a stag
and kill a boar.
The boar was huge,
the stag was speedy.
But Heracles got them,
yes, indeedy!

And now we're on
to number five,
with Heracles
still well alive.
A warning, readers,
hold your nose!
The next task's smelly.
Right, here goes…

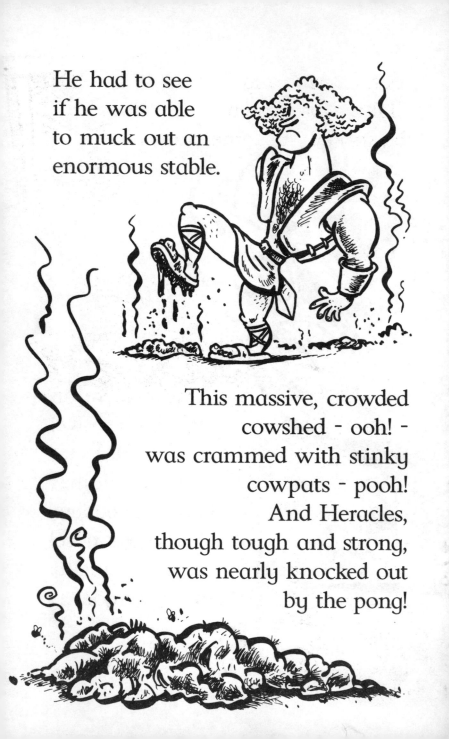

He had to see
if he was able
to muck out an
enormous stable.

This massive, crowded
cowshed - ooh! -
was crammed with stinky
cowpats - pooh!
And Heracles,
though tough and strong,
was nearly knocked out
by the pong!

But, murmuring,
"I'll not be beaten,
by something some poor
moo-cow's eaten,"
he changed a rapid
river's course
to flush the floor
with flowing force.

The river rushed
the dung away
and Heracles
put in clean hay.

And so we come to
number six,
a very different
kind of fix.

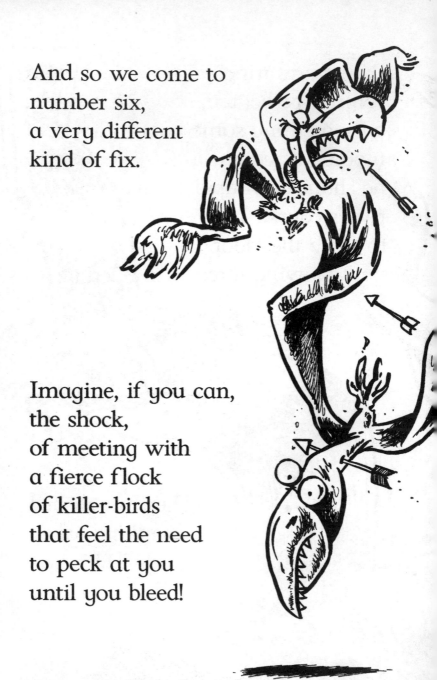

Imagine, if you can,
the shock,
of meeting with
a fierce flock
of killer-birds
that feel the need
to peck at you
until you bleed!

Heracles scared them
with a rattle,
then used his bow
to fight the battle.
He was so skilful
with that bow
they flapped and squawked
and had to go.

For seven, he sailed off
to defeat
the wild bull
that ravaged Crete.

That done, some horses
out in Thrace
were feeding on
the human race.

For speed and fury
they were famed,
but Heracles
soon had them tamed.
So, no more people
on the plate
of savage horses:
number eight.

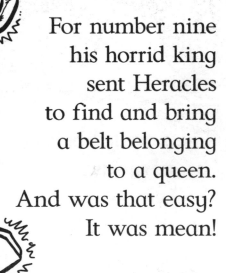

For number nine
his horrid king
sent Heracles
to find and bring
a belt belonging
to a queen.
And was that easy?
It was mean!

23

The queen, she ruled
a women's clan,
who, if they saw one,
killed a man.

The jewelled belt,
the story said,
she even wore
when tucked in bed.

24

But did our boy
use martial art
to get the belt
and queen apart?
Oh no! He made her
smile and chuckle,
and that way soon
undid the buckle.

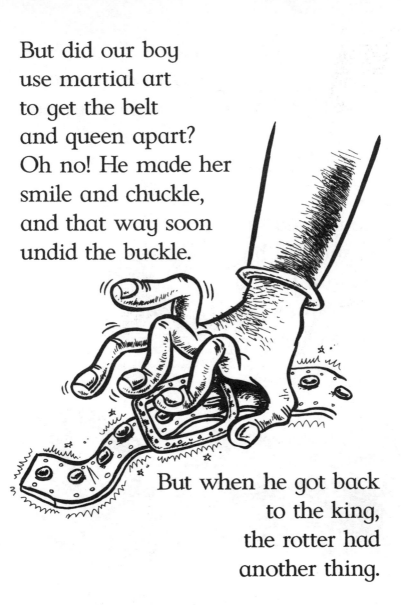

But when he got back
to the king,
the rotter had
another thing.

He said, "My boy,
your number ten
will be to find
the deadly den
that people go to
when they die.

You'll find the door
is guarded by
a giant hound
with three heads - right?
And when they're angry,
boy, they bite!"

But Heracles,
not one to squeal,
soon got the dog
to come to heel,
and took the waggy
three-tongued drooler
off to lick
his horrid ruler.

So, wiping slobber
from his eyes,
the king said,
"Out in paradise
there grows a tree
with fancy fruit -
pure golden apples,
dangerous loot!

These apples grow
upon a tree
where they are guarded
jealously
by one enormous
snake, too large
for even *you*
to shoot or charge.

They glow and glisten
in the sun.
So, off you go
and pick me one."

Our weary hero,
Heracles,
thought, "How can I
get one of these?"
But then he met
a massive guy
whose job was holding
up the sky.

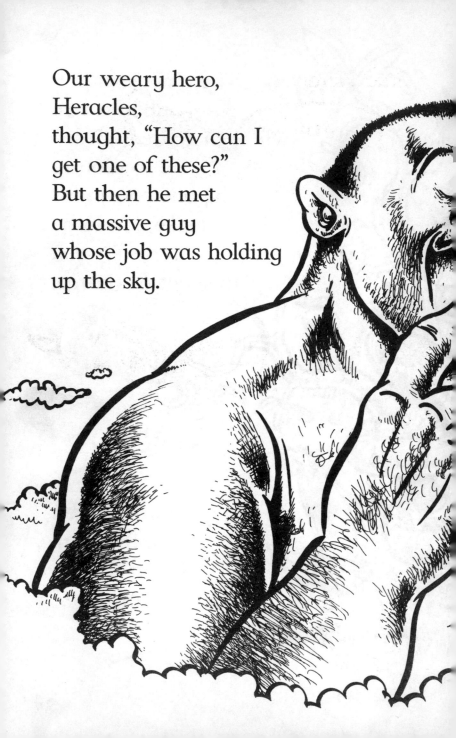

Said Heracles,

Please use your size.
While I stand in to hold your skies.

And hey, the giant brought him one! That meant our hero's tasks were done.

The golden apple
made eleven.
Then - *wow!* - get this!
Straight down from heaven
flew mighty Zeus
(that's heaven's king!)
who said, "I've watched
you do your thing
and you were great,
I'm well impressed.
So, chill out, hero,
take a rest.

Just dump that worn out
human bod.
Hang out with me
and be…a GOD!

This way Heracles
cleared the nation
to help you have
a safe vacation.
So let's be grateful
guys like this
got rid of things
that snarl and hiss.

# Brave Boy Rap

Prince Theseus
was a brave young lad.
Big bullies made him
boiling mad.
So when he heard
about a beast
whose horrid habit
was to feast
on gals 'n' guys,
he frowned, "OK!"
and went to fight it
that same day.

35

This beast was called
the Minotaur.
It lived beneath
a palace floor
upon the nearby
Isle of Crete.
It stomped about
on hooves, not feet.

Its head and shoulders
were all bull.
It also had
a tail to pull.
The rest of it
was muscle guy,
a real meanie -
true! No lie!

It spent long nights
and boring days
just sulking in
a prison maze.

Except at feed times,
when its meals
were sent to it
with shrieks and squeals.

These meals were children
sent to be
the monster's breakfast,
lunch and tea!

Prince Theseus strode up
from the shore
and knocked upon
the palace door.

He told the king
he'd come as lunch
for hungry Minotaur
to munch.
The king took Theseus
along,
then rang the monster's
dinner gong.

The king slipped off.
But just before
our hero entered
the Minotaur's door
the princess
(what a sassy girl!)
came sidling up
in quite a whirl.

She gazed at him
and boldly said,
"I hope you'll knock
that monster dead.

Now, for the maze,
you'll need this thread.
Just tie it here.
When it's unravelled
the thread will tell you
where you've travelled.
You'll find me waiting
in my coat.
I'll take you safely
to your boat.

42

My dad would kill me
if he knew
that I was down here
helping you.
But I can't stand
to see kids eaten.
It's time my dad
and his beast were beaten.

So take me with you
when you go.
I think you're gorgeous.
Good luck. Yo!"

Brave Theseus wound
his way along.
And soon he smelled
a monstrous pong.
"Phew! That must
be the Minotaur…"

He heard a swish,
a thump, a roar.
And then he saw
a big bull's head.
"You ugly dork!"
our brave prince said.

He kicked its butt
and yanked its tail.
He tweaked its ears
and made it wail.
He cried, "I'm not
a snack to scoff,"
then grabbed its horns
and pulled them off.

The rest is rather
quick to tell.
He sent the monster
straight to hell.

Then back he went
along the thread.
"Oh, well done, dude!"
the princess said.
They tip-toed lightly
to the shore,
and sailed away
for evermore.

That's all for now, folks
There you go.
Two ancient heroes.
Hunky! Yo!

# RAP RHYMES
## by Tony Mitton
### Illustrated by Martin Chatterton

**Collect all the books in this award-winning series!**

| | | |
|---|---|---|
| ❑ 1 Royal Raps | ISBN 1 86039 366 7 | £3.99 |
| ❑ 2 Big Bad Raps | ISBN 1 86039 365 9 | £3.99 |
| ❑ 3 Fangtastic Raps | ISBN 1 86039 881 2 | £3.99 |
| ❑ 4 Monster Raps | ISBN 1 86039 882 0 | £3.99 |
| ❑ 5 Scary Raps | ISBN 1 84121 153 2 | £3.99 |
| ❑ 6 Robin Hood Raps | ISBN 1 84121 157 5 | £3.99 |

**Look out for these Greek Myth Raps!**

| | | |
|---|---|---|
| ❑ 1 Mega Greek Myth Raps | ISBN 1 84121 803 0 | £3.99 |
| ❑ 2 Groovy Greek Hero Raps | ISBN 1 84121 799 9 | £3.99 |
| ❑ 3 Mighty Greek Myth Raps | ISBN 1 84121 811 1 | £3.99 |
| ❑ 4 Great Greek Myth Raps | ISBN 1 84121 807 3 | £3.99 |

*Rap Rhymes* are available from all good bookshops,
or can be ordered direct from the publisher:
Orchard Books, PO BOX 29, Douglas IM99 1BQ
Credit card orders please telephone 01624 836000
or fax 01624 837033
or e-mail: bookshop@enterprise.net for details.

To order please quote title, author and ISBN
and your full name and address.
Cheques and postal orders should be
made payable to 'Bookpost plc'.
Postage and packing is FREE within the UK
(overseas customers should add £1.00 per book).

Prices and availability are subject to change.